Little Line

A little tale
A guide for pre-writing skills
A workbook for children 3 & up

by Berenice Prado

Illustrated by Ivano Garcia

AuthorHouse™
1663 Liberty Drive
Bloomington, IN 47403
www.authorhouse.com
Phone: 1-800-839-8640

First published by AuthorHouse   11/30/2009

ISBN: 978-1-4490-3300-2 (sc)

Library of Congress Control Number: 2009910979

Printed in the United States of America
Bloomington, Indiana

This book is printed on acid-free paper.

authorHOUSE®

WHAT ARE PRE-WRITING SKILLS?

Before children learn to write, they must have a fair control of the pencil and hand skills; these are achieved by having proper strength and dexterity in the small muscles of the hands. Children also need to have good sensory information, as it tells the brain how their hands are moving and how they will coordinate motor actions. Pre-writing skills are an important component of the writing skills process, and as such, they must be stimulated according to each child's capacity.

HOW CAN I HELP MY CHILD WITH PRE-WRITING SKILLS?

Positioning

Even though a three year old would have problems sitting properly on a desk chair, it is extremely important that, even at that age, he or she starts getting into the habit of proper sitting. Your children must be encouraged to sit in a size-appropriate chair with feet flat on the floor and forearms resting on the tabletop.

Eye–Hand Coordination

Encourage activities like throwing and catching large balls, stacking, finger painting, drawing and scribbling, and playing games like Simon says. Teach up/down, back/forth, and front/back concepts during regular playtime. Use vertical surfaces for improved coordination.

Multisensory Stimulation

Good sensory processing is required to produce good coordinated work. Facilitate opportunities for input on joints and muscles to promote proximal stability and strength on upper extremities. Promote playing at playgrounds with monkey bars and ladders play tug of war, do some wheelbarrow walking, and encourage lying tummy-down on the floor with arms propped on forearms for reading and coloring. Play with Play-Do (rolling, pinching, making fingerprints, cutting with a plastic knife, and finding small hidden beads). Facilitate opportunities for children to have visual and tactile stimulation by using bright colors and different textures during tasks. Use storytelling when drawing lines and age-appropriate shapes, and do not underestimate the power of music, singing, and dancing as a preparation for pre-writing work.

The above activities are very general suggestions and are not intended to replace professional intervention. If you feel that your child struggles with some or all of these skills, you might consider contacting an occupational therapist in your area.

WHAT IS AN OCCUPATIONAL THERAPIST?

An occupational therapist is able to evaluate the underlying components that support individual handwriting abilities, such as muscle strength, endurance, coordination, motor control, and sensory processing.

Berenice Prado is a licensed occupational therapist who has a wide experience in working with children of all ages. She is an independent contractor for the school system and practices privately in the Jackson, Tennessee, area.

She can be reached at bpradoot@yahoo.com or at her Web site: www.com/Bprado/ResourcesOT.

HOW TO USE THIS WORKBOOK

Little Line has been designed with a concept of an interactive pre-writing session between the child and the caregiver (teacher or parent).

Little Line uses visual, tactile cueing, and verbalizations provided by the caregivers during the storytelling, which are extremely useful, especially when working with children with developmental disabilities, academic delays, etc. *Little Line* is ideal for basic introduction to pre-writing skills to children with clearly identified visual–motor integration challenges.

As the child is introduced to basic pre-writing concepts (lines, simple shapes, etc.), it is important to capture all of his or her attention span, which is normally very short at three or four years of age. When facilitating the *Little Line* exercises, read the little tale out loud to the child and prompt the initiation of tracing lines and forming shapes. Provide physical assistance as needed (hand-over-hand assistance, guiding the first strokes, etc.). Involve the child in the little story and remind him or her of familiar words, places mentioned in the story, colors shown, spatial relationships mentioned (up, down, to the side, big, small, etc.), and characters that the child might already know. Work throughout the book with enthusiasm; this will not only motivate the student, but it will also promote association, which will assist in the learning process.

Little Line is the one little tale and workbook that was created to promote meaningful interaction between the student and the caregiver at the time when pre-writing work takes place. We hope that *Little Line* promotes parents, teachers, and caregivers in general becoming more involved in this early stage of child development with more fun and creativity when teaching children basic concepts.

Little Line is suitable for parents seeking appropriate activities at home and for therapists working on pre-writing skills in a regular therapy session or as a recommendation for home activities to reinforce simple concepts learned at therapy. Now please join Little Line and have fun with pre-writing skills!

Sincerely,

Berenice Prado, occupational therapist

Hello!

My name is Ricky, and I want you to meet my friend Little Line.

One day when I was playing with Tony the Pencil and Peter the Paper, I found Little Line.

You can be his friend too.

All you need to do is to open this little book, and you will find all Little Line can do.

Your new friend,
Ricky

Little line stands up straight; he comes from top to bottom and stays planted on the ground like the trunk of a tree.

He stands straight, like the trunk of a tree.

Little Line can also go side to side, just like if he were to lie down on his bed.

He goes side to side to take a little rest.

After he sleeps for a while, he wants to have some fun. He goes down and looks to the side, just like the moon up in the sky.

It is so much fun that he wants to go to the other side, so he goes down and looks to the other side, and the moon is still lighting up the sky.

Little Line also knows how to go straight.

So he goes down to the side but straight, just like the falling rain.

Little Line likes the rain so much that he goes the other way to make some more rain.

But the rain soon goes away, and Little Line continues to play.

At the playground, he is able to slide away.

He goes up and down, up and down, on all the slides he finds on his way.

Little Line also goes to swim in the ocean. He swims and enjoys it as much as the rain. He goes up and down, but this time just like the ocean waves.

And at the playground, Little Line found a friend!

Little Line is now happier, because he and his friend made a new shape! Do you know what shape it is?

Now is your turn to play.

Go and find Little Line and his friends; you will see that it will blow your imagination away!

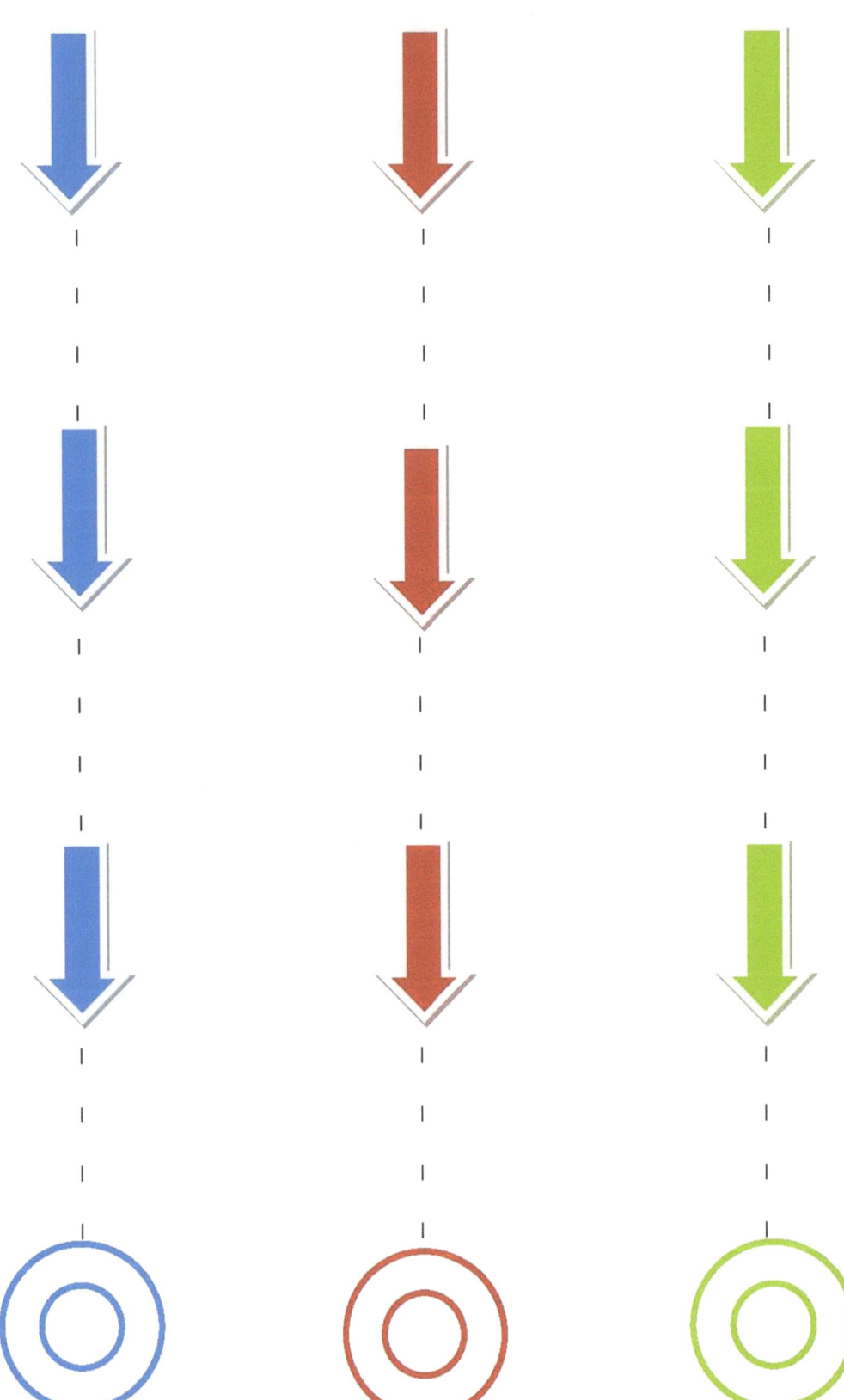

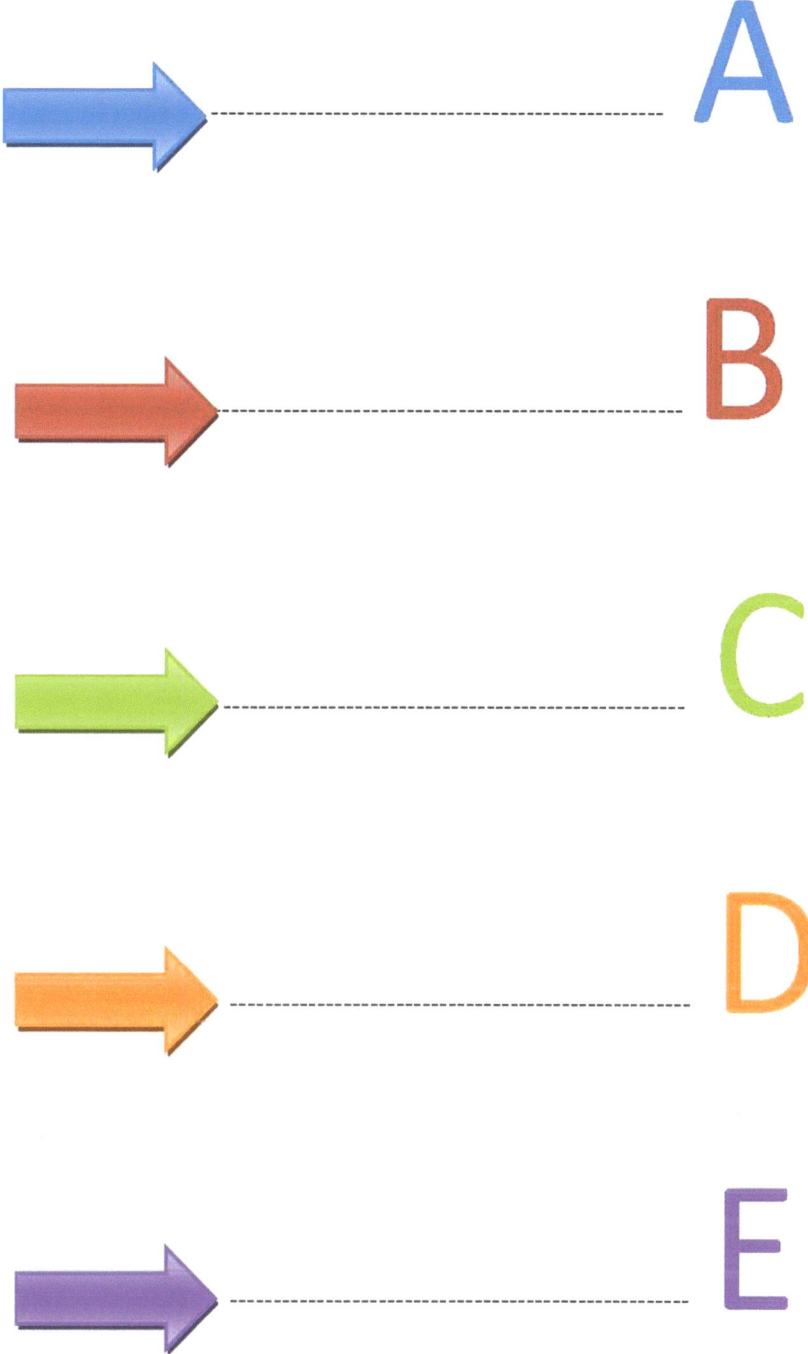

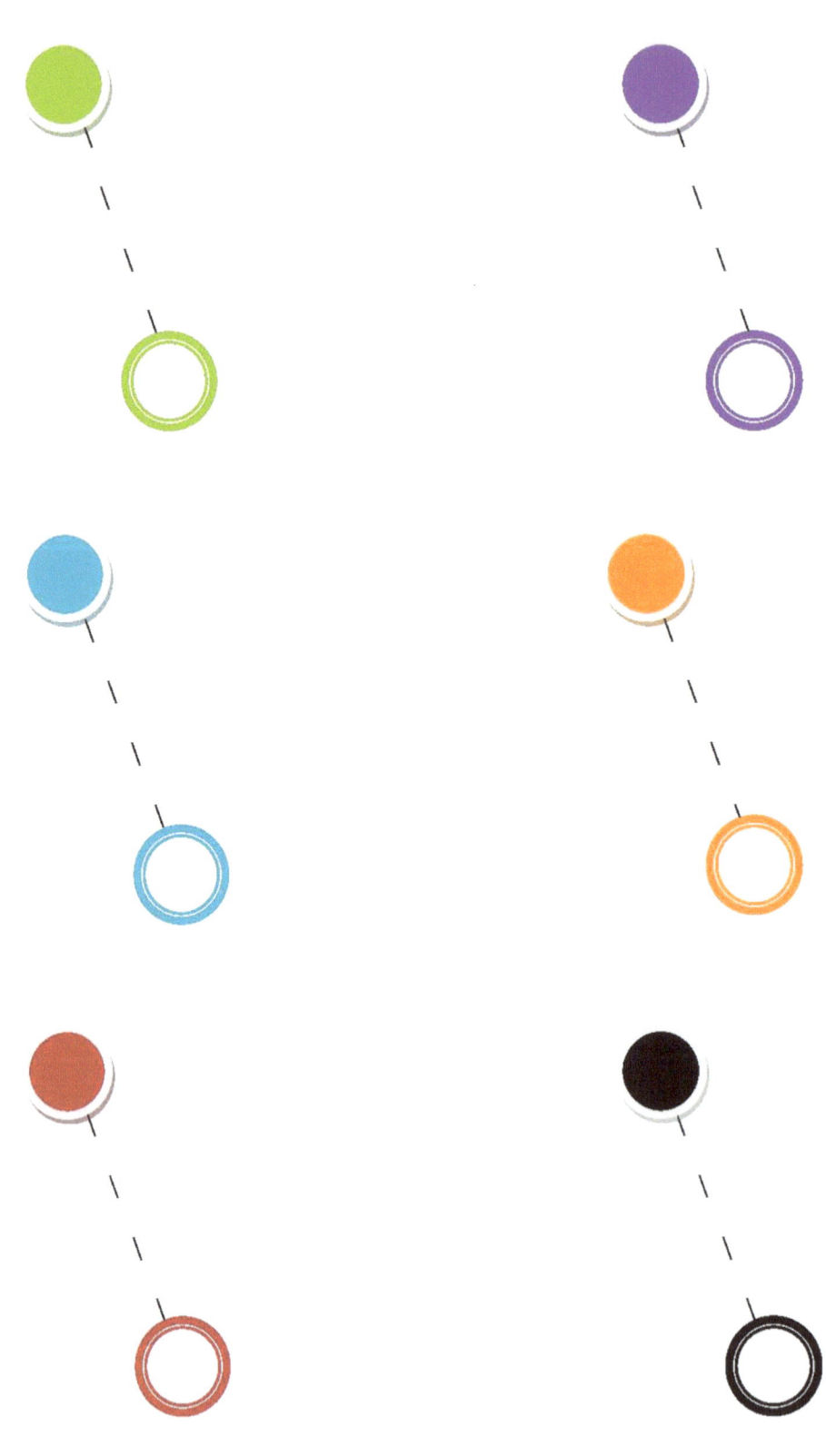

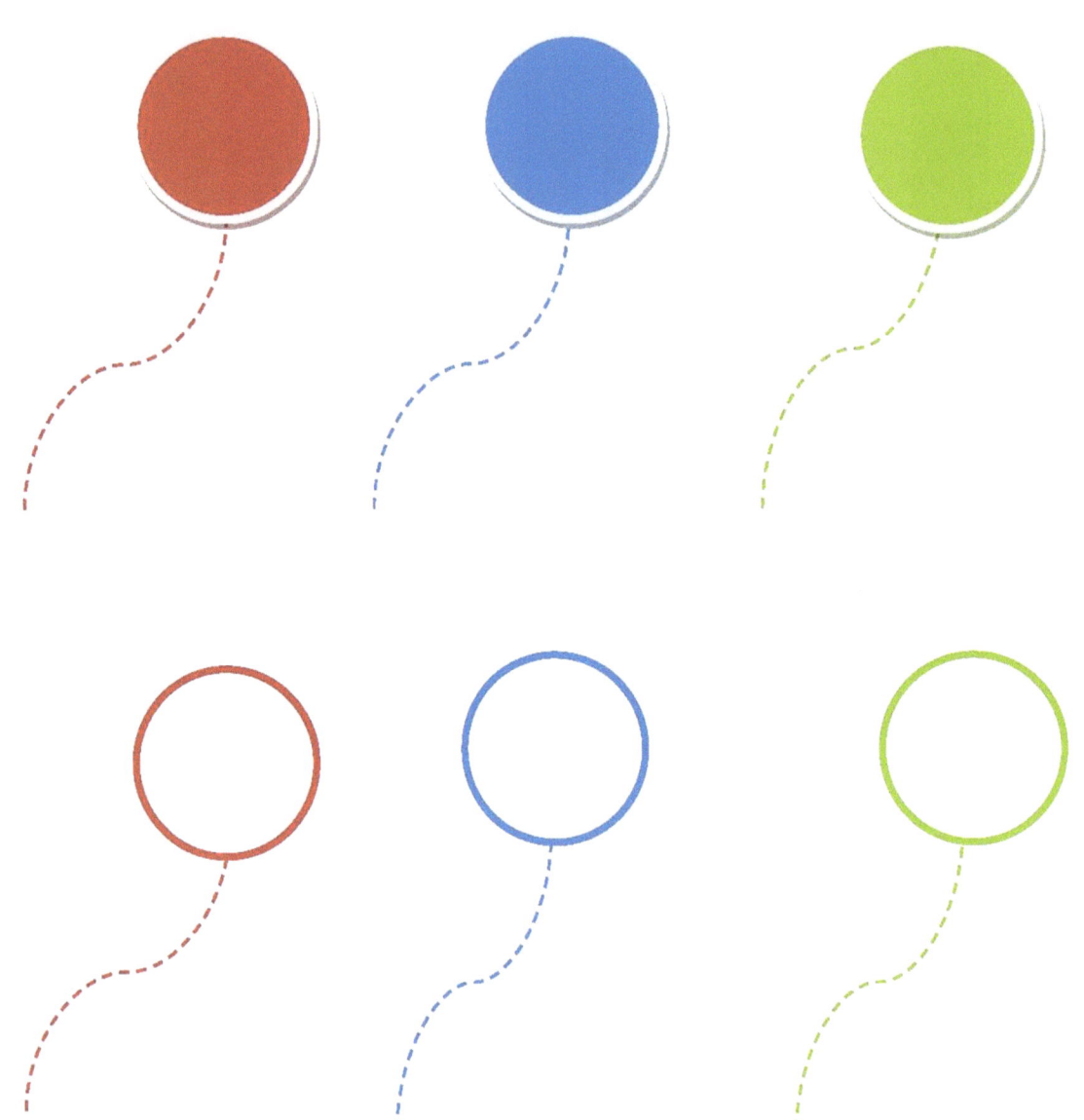

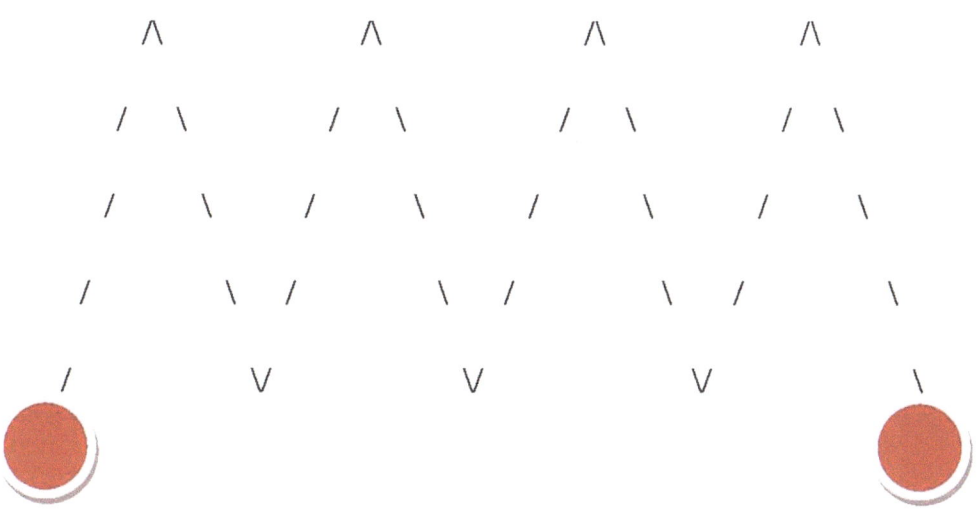

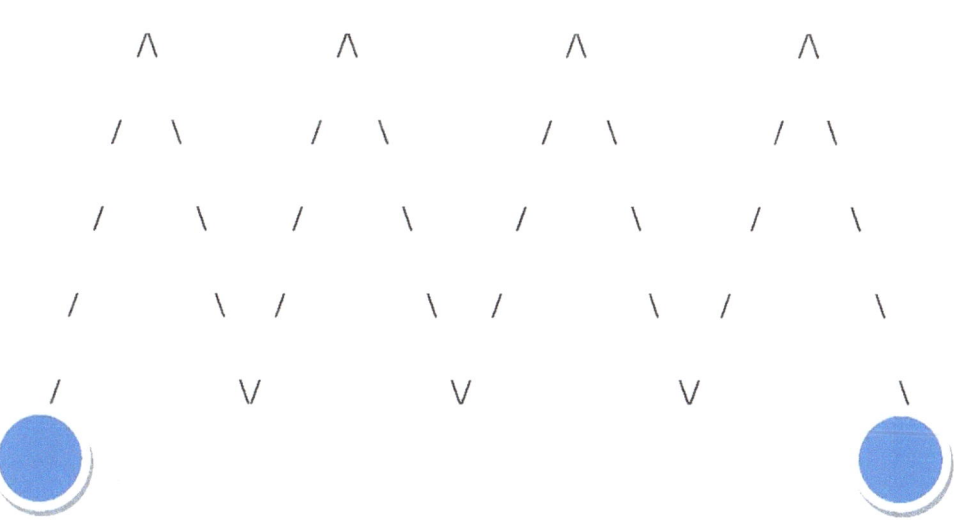

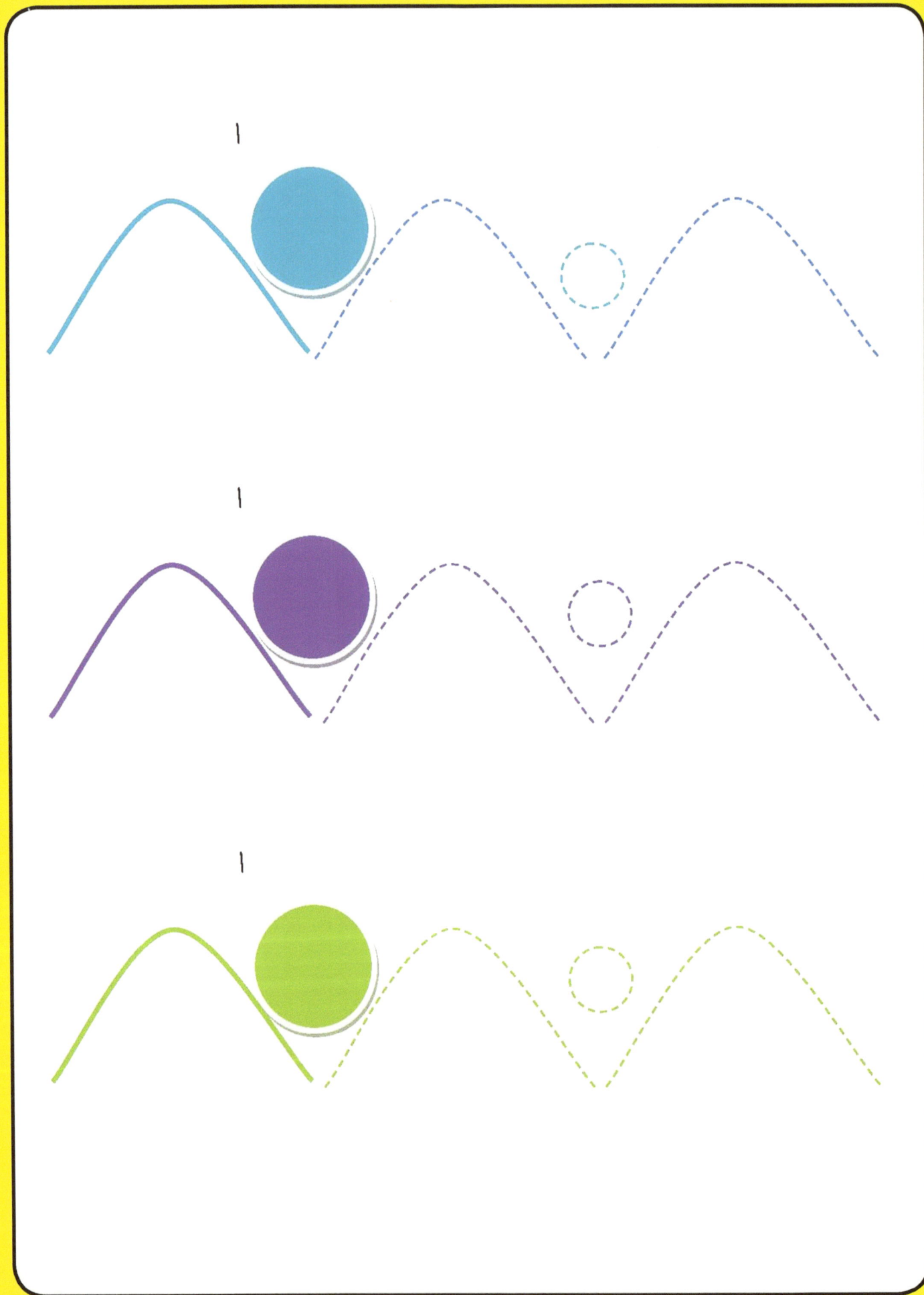

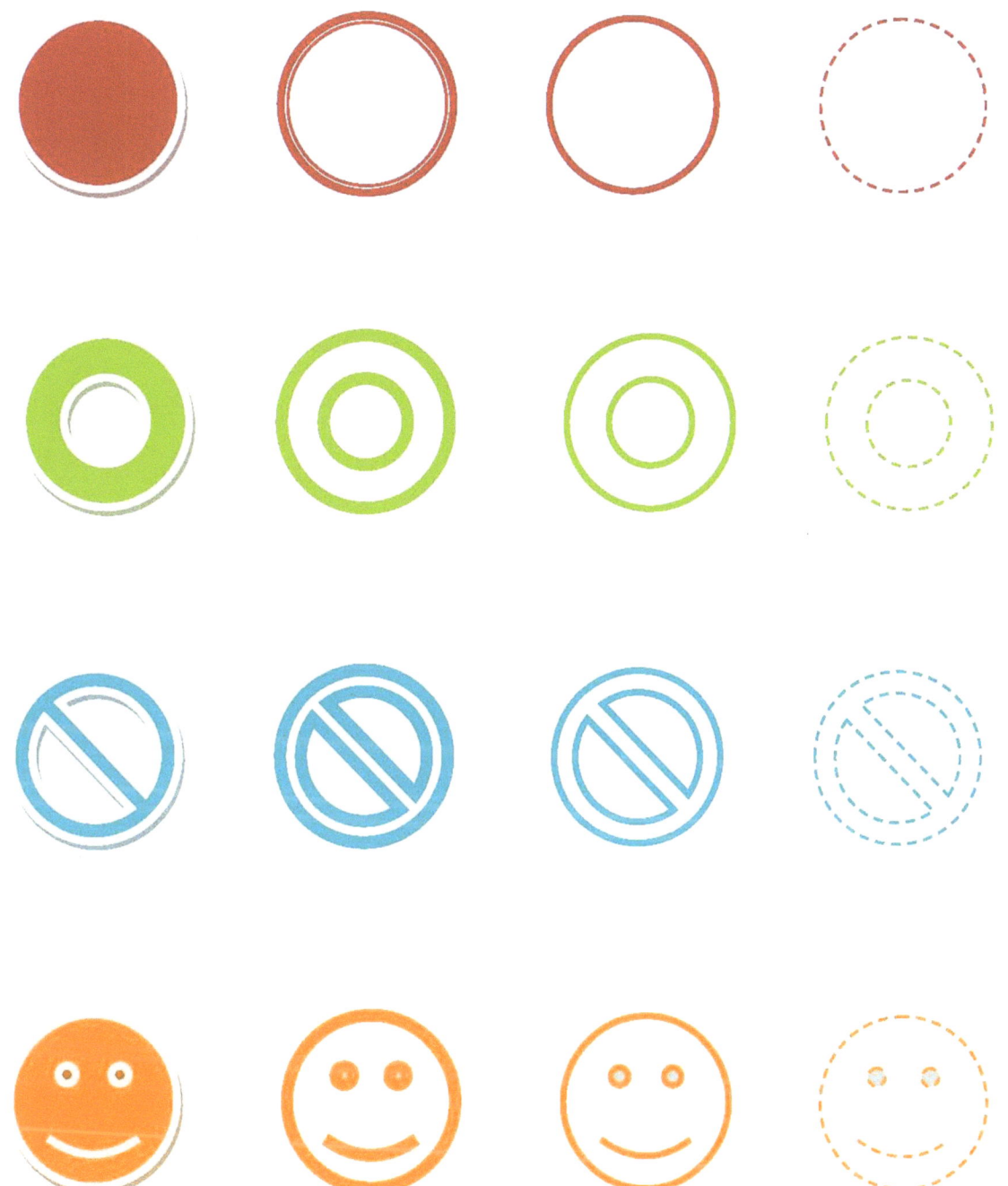

www.ingramcontent.com/pod-product-compliance
Lightning Source LLC
Chambersburg PA
CBHW060820290526

45792CB00005BB/1741